Single Black Mom's Guide to Having a Swagged-Out Lifestyle

Pamverly Green

Copyright © 2021, 2023 Pamverly Green

All rights reserved

No part of this book may be reproduced, or stored in a retrieval system, or transmitted in any form or by any means, electronic, mechanical, photocopying, recording, or otherwise, without express written permission of the publisher.

ISBN-13: 9798850246266

Cover design by: Andre Langston

Printed in the United States of America

Contents

Title Page
Copyright
Introduction

Hey Sis,	1
Stresses of Being a Mom Period	2
Dangers of Long-Term Extreme Stress	3
Added Stressors of Being Single	4
Added Stressors of Being African American	5
The Good Part:Light At the End of the Tunnel	7
Making the Vision Clear: What is Your Ultimate Goal?	8
The 3 Parts of "Being the Captain of a Happy Fulfilled Family"	9
Part One: You	11
How to Become a Swagged-Out Single Mom	12
Self-Care = Power	13
Power = Positive Energy	14
The Importance of Self-Care	16
Self-Care in YOUR Life: You Exist in 3 Parts	18
Self-Care in Physical Health	19
Eat to Live	20
Self-Care in Mental Health	22

How Meat Affects Your Mental Health	23
The Importance of Communication	24
Self-Care in Spirituality	26
You Have to Choose It	27
My Personal Experience	28
Your Natural Spiritual Place	30
Your Soul Mate Will Be Attracted to Your Light	31
Building Spiritual Health: More Fun than You Thought	32
Self-Care to the Max: The Value of Cutting Toxic People Out of Our Life	36
The Captain	37
Part Two: The Kids	38
Happy Fulfilled Kids	39
Our Kids Exist in 3 Parts Also	40
The Importance of Structure	41
The Importance of Discipline	43
Find and Invest in Your Kids' Interests	44
The Value of Natural Talents	45
Part Three:	46
Household: Needs Met and Exceeded	47
The Sum Up	49
The Conclusion	50
BONUS	53
About The Author	55

Introduction
What Does it Mean to Be a Swagged-Out Single Mom?

To be a swagged-out single mom means picking one of the topnotch versions of yourself and being that one. (Yes, Sis, there's not only a topnotch version of yourself, but an assortment of them!) A *"swagged-out" single mom* is a term that describes a mom that is living in her full potential and exuding that fullness in the quality of her and her children's lifestyle. She exercises knowledge of spiritual, mental, and physical health.

A swagged-out lifestyle is a lifestyle rich with fulfillment, connection, and functionality. For the purposes of this book, it's what we call living our best life; a righteous life. It's what we see when we imagine what a happy life would look like for us and our children. And yes, ladies, we, as single black moms, are entitled to this type of life as well.

This sounds good, right? But if you're like I was, you don't know how to make this swagged-out lifestyle your real life. This book is about to change that. Are you ready to go to the next level in your life as a parent, as a woman, and as a person overall?

With all of the drastic worldwide changes since March

2020, including the George Floyd case and COVID, it's more important than ever to get some type of "game" about yourself, ladies. "You the real MVPs!" You have the power to move yourself and your family. Let me show you how.

Hey Sis,

Let me talk to you for a minute. Girl, the saying that being a single mom is not easy is an understatement. The twists and turns required of a single mom are not for the faint at heart. Yet there are millions of us out there. There are currently 15 million single mothers in the US. And About 4.15 million of them are African American.

Stresses of Being a Mom Period

Ladies, I'm not going to sugarcoat it for you. In addition to the many blessings of motherhood, being a single mom also negatively impacts us in various ways. This impact ranges from our finances to our physical and mental health to the quality of our relationships. It can be a big pill to swallow, with some single moms often falling under the weight of depression, anxiety, excessive stress, and overwhelming fatigue.

Dangers of Long-Term Extreme Stress

The more aware we are of the stressors that we are under, the more we can strengthen ourselves against them. The problem with not dealing with stressors in life is that they create lingering negative feelings and experiences. These leave us open to a whole slew of attacks, including deteriorating self-perception, poor self-worth, and developing damaging relationships with toxic people, just to name a few. These lead us to living an overall lower quality life in general than what we want. This is usually when we start to give up our dreams and take on mindsets that damage us and our families.

This level of existence doesn't allow our children access to our best selves, which can not only limit their relationships with us but can be damaging to their overall perception of what healthy relationships are. And more importantly, this doesn't allow us access to our best selves, which is a real shame, Sis. Our best selves are where our hopes and dreams, and successes lie.

Added Stressors of Being Single

Also adding to the difficulties of parenting, is the fact that we are also still single women, which means we are on the dating scene and have the extra juggle of trying to attract a suitable mate. This entails building and maintaining an emotional relationship with a man in addition to your regular stressful duties.

And things becomes even more complicated when manipulation, dishonesty, and other painful games are introduced into the relationship, either by you or him. No matter the romantic relationship pain, though, we know all too well that momma is still expected to function in all of her usual roles. Being a mom is a full-time job that you never get to clock out from.

Added Stressors of Being African American

Then, we as black mothers must deal with the added burden of not only sexism because we are women and not valued as much as men in many jobs, but we also suffer the smothering weight of American racism. As black women, we are expected to be sex objects 24/7, with magnified attention being given to certain parts of our bodies. This, with little to no emphasis placed on our actual well-being.

Also, because we are *black,* we are often denied opportunities, taken advantage of financially, and otherwise mistreated. And although racism is painfully against us, it is also heartbreakingly against our males, who are our partners, our supports, and our sons. This leaves us alone, traumatized, and vulnerable.

And I say vulnerable, because, don't believe the hype that there is no place in your life for a man. Men are still supposed to be the protectors and providers (or co-provider, at least), even in today's society. There should be a place for the right man in your life and eventually in the same home. Marriage is still the key. Men and women have been each other's yin and yang since the beginning of time. And that is not designed to change, not even for us. Yet, persevere we must, Sis.

Humans are social creatures. Not only do we learn from each other, but it feels good to have someone's shoulder to lean on, to have a best friend that loves you, helps you carry burdens, and is down for you in general. This is a blessing. A healthy, committed relationship is a gift from God.

So, to have so many of our yangs, our men, imprisoned due to mass incarceration, killed, self-sabotaging, or otherwise have their best selves detained from us, makes our and our children's lives much more difficult. We are a yin without a yang. Single in a world where strength is more easily found in numbers, and in this case, pairs.

The Good Part: Light At the End of the Tunnel

Swagged-Out Motherhood is an Option

But, here's where it gets good. Our cases are not hopeless. Just because you have children and are single doesn't mean your regularly scheduled dreams are over. It does mean, though, that your life has drastically changed. It has become more layered. And it requires more layered skill to master. But ultimately, your dream of being happy and fulfilled with a happy and fulfilled family is very possible. This state will be further referred to in this book as "swagged-out."

With the dynamic Christian-based parenting and leadership strategies presented in this guide, you're about to learn how to become the captain of your own well-run swagged-out ship. It is possible to finally attain that accomplished parent feeling that you've always wanted, with the happy balanced family to match.

In these power-packed pages, you'll find profound, tried, and true methods that will help you learn how to find and maintain your swag as a single black mother, build real-life swag in your kids, and even attract that ideal mate in the process. Welcome to the upgraded version of yourself, girl! Let's go!

Making the Vision Clear: What is Your Ultimate Goal?

-And the Lord answered me, and said, write the vision, and make it plain. Habakkuk 2:2

In order to get the things out of life that we want, we must first be clear on what it is that we want to accomplish. What is our overall goal? This is called our vision.

The Bible says to create a vision and write it down plainly and clearly. As single moms, what we want most is what all people want, the good life. And the good life for a mom is a family and household that are functional and nurture and grow its members. Our vision is simple: **_To be the Captain of a Happy, Fulfilled Family_**. This top-of-the-line state of existence for you and your family is your swagged-out levels.

The 3 Parts of "Being the Captain of a Happy Fulfilled Family"

To realize our vision of being *the Captain of a Happy, Fulfilled Family* sounds simple enough. This type of family is fully functional and productive with a confident, knowledgeable captain. But, as we know, in reality, it's not simple at all.

To help us better grasp this abstract concept, let's break it down into 3 fundamental parts. For a highly functional family to exist, the following 3 principles must be in place. These include *(1) a happy, fulfilled mom, (2) happy, fulfilled children,* and *(3) a household where the basic needs are consistently met and exceeded.* By breaking our vision down into smaller parts, you, the kids, and your home, we can see it clearer, making it more attainable.

There is a popular saying that says *you eat the elephant one bite at a time.* It means that you can realistically reach any goal that you're trying to accomplish if you first break it down into smaller goals. Moms, remember that no matter how big your vision is, you can reach it if you break it down into smaller parts. Accomplish each part one at a time, and before you know it, you will have your heart's desires. No more need to feel intimidated. Just plan.

Speaking of reaching our vision by breaking it down into smaller parts, let's look more in depth at the 3 smaller parts of having a Happy, Fulfilled Family, which is our goal. The first and most important part of this vision is YOU and learning how to care for yourself on deeper levels.

Part One: You

How to Become a Swagged-Out Single Mom

Self-Care = Power

The Oxford Translation dictionary defines self-care as the practice of taking action to preserve or improve one's own health; and/or the practice of taking an active role in protecting one's own well-being and happiness, in particular, during periods of stress.

Of course, loving and worshipping God should come first in your life. However, part of His divine plan is for us to have a healthy respect for ourselves, His creation. Ephesians 2:10 NLT tells us that "we are God's masterpiece". Therefore, as His masterpiece, we should be dealt with with understanding and care.

Self-care is the purposeful care and culmination of yourself. This is how you can build real power in yourself. Many times we have things that we want to accomplish, but we don't have the strength or power to do so. Self-care is how you change that. It helps you become a positive energy generator for yourself!

Power = Positive Energy

To be at the top of your game, self-care is a necessity. Life is hard, and being a single black mother is even harder. With all the stressors that abound, to grow into your higher self, you'll need the ability to replenish your positive energy frequently and on demand.

Positive energy gives us power. Negative energy takes it away. In order to be swagged-out, you will need energy and motivation. These things come from power and are everyone's birthright.

By putting as much positive energy into your life as you can, you can build power in yourself. This will give you the ability to balance out the inevitable negativities that are designed to take us down. But because you have energy/power reserves, not you!

Self-care gives us ways to let the low heavy, painful vibrational pull of stress go up and out of us so that we can get back to transcending, back to cultivating our true self. Your true self, if you're meant to be swagged-out anyway.

This leads me to the fact that if you are reading this book, then the concept of being swagged-out obviously appeals to you, which means there is a high chance that you are meant to be a highly functional, fulfilled, enriching mom and person, also known as swagged-out.

Congratulations! This is great! This means that greater is not only in you but for you. You are a diamond in the rough. Now let's uncover your true self, your greater self. She lives at the core of Self-care. Let's expand our minds, ladies, around how much this concept can revolutionize our lives.

The Importance of Self-Care

As previously stated, the ultimate goal of a swagged-out single black mom is the same as all parents, to successfully captain a happy, fulfilled family. Right at the center of this vision is a happy fulfilled mom, the captain. Before much else can change in your household, be it from bad to good or from good to great, you must first see yourself as the center of this machine.

However "well oiled" it is or is not, its functioning is directly tied to you. You are the key component in a single-parent household. Think about it. Without you, nothing in your household functions properly. Without you, there is no household. So, it would stand to reason that your well-being is of the utmost importance.

Your household's health and functionality are directly related to your own. It's time to give yourself the same attention, love, acceptance, and adoration that you would give your soulmate. Because in actuality, you are the one that you always dreamed of to come and save you. Your true self. Your best version. And the only way to uncover and develop her so that she can show up and show out is through a concept called self-care. To have the life you always wanted, you must first decide that you deserve to be taken seriously and are a priority. Ladies, to reach our existence on higher levels, which is what swagged-out is, you must first adopt the concept of self-care.

Self-Care in YOUR Life: You Exist in 3 Parts

We know that self-care builds power. But, in order to care for anything effectively, you first have to understand it beyond just a surface level. This applies to ourselves as well.

First, begin by seeing yourself as you really are. You, like all human beings, are not merely physical. You are actually made up of 3 parts and exist simultaneously in all 3.

Your first part, as I just stated, is your body/physical existence. Your next part is called your soul and it consists of your mind, your emotions, and your will. Your third and most powerful part is your spirit. It is your true self and your direct connection to the Most High God.

Despite how most of us were taught, you are much more than can be seen on the outside. The Bible says you are a spirit living in a human body. And so, we are. Now, Let's explore proper care of each part of our selves.

Self-Care in Physical Health

Physically, self-care is taking care of your body. It's the part of ourselves that we are most familiar with. To ensure that we are physically healthy, we need to eat right and get regular exercise. If you have prescriptions, take them. Do your yearly physicals. Don't forget your dental health, with yearly dental check ups and cleanings every 6 months.

If you have persistent health issues, don't give up on getting relief from them. Make a conscious effort to make healthy lifestyle choices.

Eat to Live

Also, one of the best tips I can give you on having a truly "living" life is to eat living things regularly. Living things consist of fruits, vegetables, herbs, and things from the earth. You know, those things on our plate that we often neglect for the greasier, artificial, unhealthy versions of food.

Although these unhealthy foods may satisfy our tastebuds, they take your health and well-being backward and increase your chances of developing ailments that will slow you down. Ailments like heart disease, inflammation of the muscles, painful swollen joints, stomach and intestinal issues, and a whole slew of other digestion-related issues.

Physically, eating a more plant-based diet also, greatly decreases our chances of high blood pressure and diabetes, two of the main diet-related killers of Black women. It also adds health to our bodies by giving us more energy, helping with weight loss, clearing up skin, helping us heal faster, and many other great things.

I know the struggle is real, girls. But the benefits are undeniable. And eating to live, not living to eat, is a characteristic of a swagged-out mom.

And I do know that even with all this information about the benefits to our physical health of eating more living things (and less dead things, like meat, junk food, etc.), it can still be hard to make the right decisions. So, consider this. We know that eating living things is good for our bodies, but did you also know that eating living things is good for your mind? Which takes us into the next realm of our existence, our mental/emotional health.

Self-Care in Mental Health

Sis, we are not often told of the effects of eating living things on our minds. But the same way that our bodies work at optimal performance with healthy food and regular exercise is the same way our minds do too. A living creative mind is quick and can literally create beneficial logical solutions that weren't there before." Quicken me, O Lord, according unto thy word!" (Psalm 119:107, KJV.

Total health for human beings cannot exist without care being given to our minds as well. The importance of our mental and emotional health deserves to be highlighted more. This is particularly true in the African American community, where we have not traditionally talked about mental health.

How Meat Affects Your Mental Health

For extended benefits, consider decreasing or altogether eliminating your meat intake, especially red meat. Eliminating red meat from your diet in addition to being healthy for your body, will also help you gain more emotional control and stability, stronger focus, increased mental clarity, and greater feelings of overall well-being. It may seem like a lot, to give up or even limit your meat intake, but the benefits are undeniable.

The Importance of Communication

On average, people provide and receive mental help from each other all the time, through communication. Your voice is a very powerful tool. The Bible tells us that the power of life and death lies in our tongue. Use your voice to speak your truth. Tell your story. And in real life this means, talk.

Talk to those that care about you and your real feelings. Talking to the right people about our problems will relieve stress and also opens us up to receiving advice on making it better from someone that cares about our well-being. Accept the fact that hurt people hurt people. So, take care of yourself.

Providing mental health to yourself is important too. It can be as small as listening to your favorite song uninterrupted while in the bathroom or as complex as seeking out professional counseling or psychiatric help in cases when severe emotional damage and blockages are present. Providing mental health to yourself means learning your boundaries and proactively bringing positivity into your life to keep your mind balanced.

What kind of things are you doing to bring joy and peace to your mind? Our emotions are just as real as our bodies. Both are susceptible to getting sick if not cared for properly, getting scar tissue from traumatic injuries, and getting hurt immensely when broken. The only difference is one is visible, the other invisible.

Do whatever righteous things it takes to resolve unresolved hurt and move on at peace in your life. At the end of the day, it truly is for your own freedom, not for others.

Self-Care in Spirituality

As we now look at the third part of us, our spirit, let us be mindful that our spirit is our most powerful part and has the ability to transform the other 2 parts. Spiritual cultivation, the purposeful development of your spirit, is a requirement of a swagged-out single black mother. In your spirit is where lies your character, the kind of person you are, your personality, your hopes and dreams.

So, with that being said, ladies, let me make it clear that, yes, your spirit is real. All your life, that part of you has never aged. It's never changed. Your spirit is the highest part of you where your direct connection to the Most High God is.

You Have to Choose It

Cultivating your spirit is the key to overcoming emotional and physical scar tissue, renewing your strength, and maintaining a "swagged-out" level of existence. But make no mistake about it, Sis, you have to choose God. Spiritual growth first requires you to submit yourself to the idea that God is in control, not you. And that He loves you and wants what's best for you.

Know that He believes that you are so valuable that he sent his son, Jesus Christ to not only teach you how to live your best life, a Godly life, but to bleed and die for you so that you might have a chance to be redeemed. 1 Corinthians 6:20 says you were bought with a price which mean you belong to Him. Living for God, He will hold the pressure for you and show you how to stand.

My Personal Experience

I experienced this personally when I was 20 years old. I decided to try meditation for the first time right before a planned suicide attempt. Beyond obvious reasons, this meditation time changed my life.

From what unexpectedly grew into a 30-minute meditation session, I remember opening my eyes, and the crippling anxiety that had held me captive in my house from undiagnosed Generalized Anxiety Disorder and Social Phobia was gone. The suffocating depression that had just written my suicide note was gone. The anguish associated with these disorders that had kept me from attending classes for months was no longer there when I opened my eyes. I couldn't believe it!

I was generally terrified in the presence of wide-open spaces with groups. So, I often drove to class and illegally parked in front of the buildings so I could get in and out quickly. But when the cost of the tickets threatened my tuition, I was forced to walk.

Walking was difficult because it was much more uncontrolled, exposed, and downright painful to endure. My heart beat out of my chest for the entire 10 minutes. I sweated. I breathed shallowly. My stomach and cest were tight. I was terrified.

I was afraid to make eye contact with anyone. And when I finally got to class, sometimes I still couldn't calm down. So, I would sit there, trying to appear calm and disappear into the background. All while feeling like a bear was chasing me for 45 to 95 minutes, over and over again. After a while, it wore thin, and I broke mentally. That's when I stopped going altogether that year.

But not that day. Not this meditation day. That day, I went to every class. I strutted across that huge college campus with a lightness and confidence that I hadn't felt since I moved off campus alone over 6 months prior. Today the spirit of triumph existed in the place of intimidation, shame, and terror. I was ecstatic. This was the first time I consciously saw a connection between God and my "real-life" well-being. But it wouldn't be the last.

3 days later while doing my hair in the bathroom mirror, the words came to my mind like a thought that I had remembered, "God is real. And lives inside of You!" It soaked into my mind like, "Oh, yea, I had forgot that," and within seconds it came down through my body in waves of knowing. I knew that this was true and that I had been mistaken all my life. God didn't just live up in the clouds. He lived in us. In me. Therefore, I could talk to Him and hear Holy Spirit talk back. We could literally do anything through Christ who strengthens us. We did not have to suffer! I was elated and thankful for this information and knew it came from the spirit realm. That's when I first chose God because He chose me.

Your Natural Spiritual Place

During my spiritual revelation in college, God taught me that my natural place is with Him. No matter, how advanced or independent I believed I was, He taught me that in reality, I am only a branch, and He is the tree. And when I am in my place, it feels oh so good, and things work together well. So, if you have the desire to be a great mom and person, then being a branch of God's glorious vine is your place too.

A real relationship with God is one where He responds to your prayers. Yes! Prayer is part of a real conversation with God. He shows you how to serve Him through talking to you and through the reading of His word, the Bible. But more on that later.

When you come into agreement with God, your life works. It fits. It functions well. As you seek to learn more about yourself, to move closer to your true self, you will find that you will also be moving closer to God. You will feel it.

Your Soul Mate Will Be Attracted to Your Light

In the spiritual realm, we start to understand that as our true selves, we are a star. When we provide self-care to all 3 of our parts, we shine out brightly. In this state, we are very attractive.

When you are *shining out* from your spirit, people that are for you will see you. This includes your soul mate. He will feel you. And he will pursue you.

Proverbs 18:22 tells us that "Whoso findeth a wife findeth a good thing, and obtaineth favour of the Lord". So let your light shine, shine, shine, girl! And be selective with who you allow to enjoy your light.

Building Spiritual Health: More Fun than You Thought

Growing yourself spiritually, which means developing a relationship with God and growing your character, is not nearly as hard as you may believe. And, ladies, I do understand that in the world we live in today, spiritual growth usually doesn't make the top 10 list of things that we feel are causing problems in our lives. But I'm telling you that taking the time to develop your spiritual life is the gift that keeps on giving. It propels you right into swagged-outness.

Investing in yourself spiritually doesn't mean you have to reinvent the wheel. There are some simple tried and true methods that will give you a lot of bang for your buck. The overall idea is to give yourself as many positivity injections as you can.

Ways to Grow Yourself Spiritually:

- ♦ Music Me, Please!

    Start with something you already enjoy. Music ,in general, is a great way to release stress and take your mind to a freer happier place. It can be inspiring music of your choice and/or Gospel music.

    For me, when I'm really stressed and *going through,* as they say, I like old-school, down- south. Mississippi-style gospel. You know, the kind momma and grandma *'nem* used to listen to.

I go deeper by paying attention to the lyrics and the music tone. This helps me feel that I am not alone and that I have the option of trusting in God. You have this same option too, Sis.

Gospel music was created by African Americans to help us find power for endurance. That's why spirituals were often sang during the Civil Rights Movement marches and protests. Know that you too are capable of getting through your particular rough times just like your grandmas did before you.

- Prayer and Spiritual Meditation

    Spiritual meditation and prayer should go hand in hand. Prayer allows you to talk to The Most High God. He tells us to constantly pray to Him to let Him know our concerns and needs because he cares about us and can help us. When you pray, talk to Him like He's your daddy because He wants a relationshiop with you, which means He wants you to be real with Him. Prayer to the living God truly does change things.

    Spiritual meditation allows you to listen back for God's answers. There are many Christian ways to meditate spiritually. One of my favorites is giving deep thought to a particular passage of scripture or spiritual concept. As you focus on the concept, you allow God access to your mind, giving yourself the opportunity to receive guidance and plans.

When I meditated in college and had the awakening I mentioned earlier, I did an even simpler method. I sat "criss-cross apple sauce" on the floor, closed my eyes, and focused on my breathing. I imagined my breath coming in my nose, down my throat, into my lungs, then back up and out my mouth, over and over again. This freed my mind up for Holy Spirit to take control.

Spiritual meditation and prayer are you giving yourself chances to connect with God to download new information, new energy, new purpose, extended vision, etc. Real swagged-outness comes from being guided from within, by Holy Spirit.

- Going to Church post Corona

    For spiritual growth develop a system of frequent positive Christain inpour into yourself. This should include weekly sermons. I recommend Apostle Tony Wade of Divine Life Church, Vlad Savchuk or Stephanie Ike. All are extraordinary teachers and are on YouTube.

    You should also find a church to attend physically. In addition to spiritual teachings, attending a church physically has the added benefit of positive social activities and support for both you and your children.

- At-Home Bible Study

Do home bible studies with yourself and your kids once a week. You already have access to the textbook. It's the Holy Bible. I usually use the KJV version. I'm old-school. But either version is fine.

It's as easy as reading 1-5 verses and then briefly personally analyzing them for meaning. (Google can help.) Once they are clear to you, read them with your kids and discuss their meaning. The whole processdoesn't have to take more than 30 minutes.

This *simple* act will impact your entire life. Not only will developing your knowledge of the ways of The Most High God help you and your children develop your character and learn strategies to allow you to persevere into your swagged-out lifestyle, but God's word has transformative powers. It's literally medicine for your soul. Spiritual development and growth is the name of the game.

Self-Care to the Max: The Value of Cutting Toxic People Out of Our Life

Self-care is based on the belief that you have value and deserve to be treated properly. Self-Care says I agree with the fact that every human being has value, including myself. And what is considered decent treatment for others is the same decent treatment that I also require.

Self-care says I agree with the Bible when God says "I bought you with a price" and "I knew you before you were born". A very powerful self-care guideline is to cut toxic people out of your life.

Toxic people are people that purposely hurt others emotionally/ mentally, and/or physically, for their own gain. They consistently add negative feelings to our lives. Toxicity is usually a side effect of thinking poorly of one's self. Even at their best attempt, a toxic person will continue to hurt you with the same negative competitive demeaning behaviors. They may say, and at times, act as if they have changed. In some cases, they may even believe this to be true themselves. But in the long run, when the pressure is on, a true toxic person won't be able to resist ways to be themselves, and it will always be at your expense. Learn to *cut your grass low*, Sis. So, you can see the snakes that've been hiding there.

The Captain

You are the key ingredient of your vision. A happy, fulfilled mom is at the center of a happy, fulfilled family. You are the captain. We now know that taking care of ourselves is how we take care of our families. By making sure that we not only last but that our best self is the one that is lasting, we provide our children with a model of a parent with confidence, wisdom, and integrity and a household that supports this elevated state of existing. This is how we truly teach our children how to go out into the world and hold their own. So, let's look at the second part of a Happy Fulfilled Family, the kids.

Part Two: The Kids

Happy Fulfilled Kids

Good feelings come from seeing our children be successful. And being successful builds confidence. Confidence, moms, is necessary to move things in the world. It's a big part of the positive power we discussed earlier. We can raise our children with strategies, or ways of doing things, to help them better build positive power and more effectively overcome negative things in life.

Our children are a permanent fixture in our lives. Their thoughts, moods, and actions are greatly affected by us, and us by them. So, it is to the benefit of everyone to deal with a happy, productive child as opposed to an unhappy, destructive one. But trust me, girl, without discipline, structure, and productivity, your kid won't know the difference. As the old folks say, *if you don't teach them discipline now, somebody will (the police or the grave).*

Now is more important than ever to purposely teach our kids how to cultivate a happy, fulfilled life in their own swagged-out style. This detrimental difference in individual growth is literally the difference between life and death.

Our Kids Exist in 3 Parts Also

All effective parents care about the well-being of their children. A swagged-out single mom is an emotionally mature parent that recognizes that her children not only have physical needs (food, water, shelter, clothing, medicine, etc.), but like her and all other people, they also have mental needs and spiritual needs. They, like us, make the most gains when all 3 parts are in working order.

The Importance of Structure

First, happy children are fulfilled children. Fulfilled children are confident children. Confident children have high self-esteem and believe that they can reach attainable goals. This ability is built through structure and discipline.

Structure is certain things happening at certain times, basically routines and schedules. Our jobs run this way. We have a set time (and method) to clock in. A set time (and method) to clock out. And very specific goals to accomplish with each part of our workday. Because of the highly structured nature of the work day, workers are able to meet the daily demands and goals required of them to be productive on the job.Our children and households run best on this same model.

Having routines in place not only helps your household run smoother, but also teaches kids responsibility and build self-esteem. Routines also add a natural pattern to the day and help ensure that all of your child's needs are met. Needs like nutrition, (meal and snack times), quality time (Family game/movie night), educational time (documentaries or reading), spiritual time (Bible Study), proper rest (bedtimes) and house cleaning (chores), just to name a few.

Encourage your kids to be independent, responsible, and successful at home by structuring their days so that they can get the most benefit out of them. Using time wisely is how successes are built, at home, at work, and in the world in general.

At home successes build in public confidence and self-esteem. So, decide what's important to you for your kids to get accomplished while also building character. Then get your routines and schedule going. You and your kids deserve nothing less than yawl's best, girl!

The Importance of Discipline

Structure is maintained through discipline. Discipline is defined as a process by which one learns a set of rules. Discipline entails setting clear expectations, or rules, for our kids and holding them accountable for them. We do so with real consequences and rewards to teach them behavior. Being consistent with our rules and routines is the basis of discipline. it teaches integrity, independence, and the value of hard work. Biblically, the process by which God's people learned obedience was the "discipline of the Lord" (Deuteronomy 11:2 NIV)

Providing children with discipline helps them attain goals not only now but in the future as well. Being familiar with discipline and structure will help them know how to attain even bigger goals. Attaining Big goals in life is really what being fulfilled and swagged-out is all about.

Self-discipline is required by single mothers to keep the structure for themselves and their household. This is hard and why self-care is a necessity to help us maintain ourselves. Children require structure. They'll never ask for it, but they love it. It is our responsibility to discipline ourselves enough to provide it for them.

Find and Invest in Your Kids' Interests

A swagged-out single mom wants her kids to be swagged-out too. So, in addition to basic structure and discipline (set time and space for homework, art time, family exercise, etc.), she also extends structure to shaping her kids towards activities around their specific interests.

Being involved in any positive activities i.e., gymnastics, basketball, taekwondo, church activities, etc.) are beneficial to kids' self-esteem and mental health. However, we can actually go a step higher by involving our children in a positive activity that also has a special interest to the child. This is a way to teach your child self-value, self-concept, and how to develop parts of themselves that we refer to as their natural talents.

The Value of Natural Talents

Natural gifts. Believe it or not, Sis, we all have them. Allowing our kids access to activities that match their natural interests will help them develop these gifts and move closer to their true selves. In Proverbs 18:16, the bible says, "A man's gift maketh room for him, and bringeth him before great men."

For your kids' sake, remember that they are already born with certain gifts. We all are. These are things that we are naturally interested in. Things we would do for free. Who knew that the talents you've expressed since you were a child are the very things that were given to you to help bring you your fortune! This is what is called natural law. It will always be true through eternity.

These lessons in self-respect and perseverance will help them have more success right now, from day to day. And remember, a swagged-out single black mom is only as swagged-out as her kids. So, we take A1 care of ourselves so we can provide A1 care for them.

Part Three:

Home Environment

Household: Needs Met and Exceeded

Now onto, the third and final part of attaining our vision of having a happy, fulfilled family. With yourself and your kids squared away, the only thing left is your household. Household refers to your physical home and the culture in it. A healthy household has an environment where the needs of the physical home and the needs of each member are met and exceeded.

We can better monitor these needs by breaking our household and its environment down into smaller parts. In this type of household, (1) members are physically safe, (2) the household is financially stable, (3) the good health, in all 3 of its aspects, of all members is a priority, (4) there is good communication between members, and (5) a spiritual connection is established. A spiritual connection comes with a plan of regular spiritual growth where access is granted to spiritual growth material.

Being swagged-out entails severing as many negative ties as possible to unnecessary things that pull us down, or as the bible says, "bind" us, and replacing them with positive ties. Positive ties allow us to enjoy higher-level things in life, the gifts of the spirit.

As we know, with kids, the unpredictable is always an option. But taking steps to balance these key parts of your household can help propel you and your family to success. Creating a balanced nurturing culture in our homes is our way of stacking the odds in our and our kids' favor. So, you and your family may go out into the world and not be permanently stopped by negativity. This means yawl can keep rising, Sis. Together.

The Sum Up

The strategies presented in this guide will help you get more of the things that you want out of life and reach every parent's dream of being the captain of a Happy, Fulfilled Family. Caring for yourself and your family is the key. Study these principles and give yourself, your kids, and your household ample time and space to develop these concepts over time. Don't be too hard on yourself. And remember, the most important thing is to keep moving. Love Yourself. Be resilient, even on the hard days...and keep moving.

The principles in this guide will help you to push through. To endure. These are the keys to a swagged-out lifestyle. I hope you can now see that it is possible to tell the devil to get under your feet all your life. Tell him to take several seats by being self-renewing by practicing the principles you've learned in this guide.

I truly hope this work of love was a blessing to you, Sis. I wanna see all moms win because when moms win, kids, families, and communities win too. And in those cases, the Most High is glorified. Peace and prosperity be unto you, or should I say I wish swagged-outness to you all, ladies! One Luv

The Conclusion

Salvation. The Secret to Being Swagged-Out Forever

In all honesty, I have already said that Jesus is my swag. He is everything good and strong about me. He is every part of me that has ever overcome. You see, I am a true believer in Him, which means I am saved. This means I accept Jesus Christ as my personal Lord and Savior. This doesn't mean that I am perfect or that my life doesn't have pain or suffering. After all, the bible says that we all fall short of the glory of God and that pain and suffering are parts of living in this world.

What being saved does mean is that I am saved from the condemnation and judgment of sin. So, remarkably, I am going to live forever in heaven with God! I can also count on His omnipotence to help me stand and find peace in the hardships of this life. In Psalms 91:2, we see that God is our refuge and our fortress. If I stay with Him, I am never permanently broken. I am never truly defeated. 1 John 4:4 says that *I am of God and have overcome them already, because greater is He that is in me than he that is in the world.* If you accept Him as your Lord and Savior, this is also true of you, Sis.

Romans 10:9-10 says *If you declare with your mouth, "Jesus is Lord," and believe in your heart that God raised him from the dead, you will be saved. For it is with your heart that you believe and are justified, and it is with your mouth that you profess your faith and are saved.*

Now is the time in your life to step out on faith and reclaim your victory. Your God-given purpose. Your real swag. It's free. It's very simple. And you can do it right now!

Pray this prayer, Sis.

Dear God,

I know that I am a sinner and have fallen short of your purpose for my life. I have not put you first in my life or in my heart. I come to you today, asking for your forgiveness of all my sins in the name of Jesus Christ. Jesus, I ask you to come into my heart right now. I confess that You are the son of God and that You died and rose from the dead for my sins so that I could have a chance to be redeemed. You are my Lord and Savior.

I ask for the gift of Holy Spirit to guide me on this path so that I may walk closer to you. In Your word, You said Whom the Son sets free is free indeed. Thank you, Jesus, for setting me free. I am Saved. Hallelujah!

How wonderful that you've taken this big step in your life! Luke 15:10 says that the angels in heaven are rejoicing right now on your behalf! Continue to allow yourself to receive "food" from God. Your spirit is now saved. But the rest of you will need to be fed His word to continue growing in this new direction.

In the Building Spiritual Health section of this guide, I talk about attending church and doing at-home bible study. Revisit this section. Hearing God's word is important. Romans 10:17 says that *faith cometh by hearing, and hearing by the word of God*. Not only is the bible the greatest book of wisdom ever written, but God's word is also living and is literally medicine to your soul.

There are several apps that can assist with reading the bible. My favorite is called "YouVersion Bible App + Audio" by Life.Church. It can be downloaded on any device. I also encourage you to find a church home. If you are in the Memphis area, Divine Life Church pastored by Apostle Tony Wade, is a great option. Stay connected. God is with you, Sis! And remember, although weapons will form against you (and try you) none shall prosper! (Isaiah 54:17). All praises to the Most High God!

Bonus

How To Be Resilient: The Raised Chain Link Symbol

While working on my upcoming book, When the Walls and Floors Move, God sent me a dream. In the dream, He showed me the key to resilience. It was a way of understanding that helps with overcoming obstacles. I understood it to be in the form of what I call an extended Chevrolet symbol. (See Diagram A at the end of this section).

Meaning of the Raised Chain Link Symbol

1. At first, life is straight. Good. That's the beginning, the skinny part of the symbol. 2. Then, as life stressors, including emotional stressors and other negative factors, apply themselves to our life, things can feel out of control or "thick" if you will. This is the thick middle part of the symbol.

But God says 3. No matter the feeling of the thickness, keep moving, keep going. Keep your energy flowing forward as best you can. And you will come out on the other side of the thickness, get through the stress and get straight again, back to the narrow part of the symbol. Your regular life.

And all through your life, repeat steps 1 through 3. The way is to not be broken, or perform at half the level, but to endure and push past the negative forces and perform at your full level. As you work to perform at your full level, you will push negativity's power out of your life in general and become resilient.

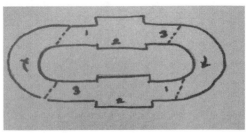

About The Author

Pamverly Green

Pamverly Green is a teacher and a writer in Memphis, TN. She attained her Bachelor of Arts Degree in Psychology from the University of Mississippi (Ole Miss) in 2001. While there, she became interested in activism and human rights. After graduation, she started a career in social services assisting troubled youth and families.

In 2007, she completed her Master of Arts Degree in Teaching in Instruction and Curriculum Leadership at the University of Memphis becoming an elementary teacher. During her 12-year career, she served as a teacher and school librarian. After completing her Administrator's License in 2017, she also served as interning vice principal at a day treatment facility for emotionally disturbed youth.

She is also the proud mom of a 7 year-old daughter.

Made in the USA
Columbia, SC
29 September 2023